Superfoods

Healthy, Nourishing and Energizing Recipes

WHITE STAR PUBLISHERS

Photographs and Recipes
CINZIA TRENCHI

Project Editor
VALERIA MANFERTO DE FABIANIS

Graphic Design
MARIA CUCCHI

INTRODUCTION

The Properties of Basic Foods and How to Use Them

STARTERS AND APERITIFS

FIRST COURSES AND SINGLE DISHES

The recipes

Introduction

Chili, eggs, extra virgin olive oil, flour, garlic and pepper: these are some of the "essential" ingredients usually available in every kitchen. We now discover that they, protagonists of innumerable recipes which are part of our everyday diet, are able, with others, to make the difference!

Never before have food and good health been so topical for everyone: they involve anyone who is a little careful about his/her well-being. Thus food is transformed into an ally and, above all, when we eat we can think about improving our quality of life! So this is how we form the concept of "superfood", but what exactly is it about? Are these foods with extreme qualities? Are they genetically modified? Definitely not. The new orientations encourage us towards healthier food, if possible from seasonal organic farming. The intrinsic qualities of foods, in fact, emerge in these kind of crops thanks to their following the natural rhythms of the earth's rotation. Superfoods are just this: food that nature has enhanced by supplying suitable nutrition for natural adaptation to the various moments of the year. Fresh juicy tomatoes, for example, are perfect for the summer, as are all the summer vegetables and fruit that help us to bear the scorching heat, while cabbage, turnips, potatoes, and legumes (low in water) are perfect for helping us in the winter months.

However, this is only one aspect: garlic is a powerful tonic in cases of fatigue, it helps to fight off colds, and fights the "bad" cholesterol (LDL). The humble Swiss chard, green spinach, aromatic arugula, delicious cauliflower, captivating carrots, are only some of the vegetables which, together with buckwheat, wheat, chickpeas, millet, beans and soy, can take us on a journey towards the cuisine of the future. A cuisine that combines diets from gastronomic customs from all over the world, providing not only taste and nutrition, but also guidance, which stamps the passport to awareness in health.

Among the superfoods we can find apparently poor food, like oily fish: not the great and important ones, tuna and swordfish for example, but anchovies, sardines, mackerel, which are rich in Omega 3 and not expensive! Besides the numerous advantages, superfoods are affordable for everyone and are part of the dietary tradition. Therefore, these kinds of food are familiar, with tastes that belong to everyone's culinary memory. Of course, there are some exceptions, which lead us to discover the wonders of far-away countries, like Goji berries, which come from Mongolia giving us anti-fatigue qualities and which fight tiredness. But how can we make use of elements we know little about? Let's introduce them carefully, in small quantities, to discover, without any distress, how our body reacts to new foods. For berries, for example, it is advisable not to exceed about 30 grams a day, and not daily.

From macrobiotics we take cereals and seeds, derived from the Japanese tradition: soy, tofu, miso, azuki beans, seaweed, food which most people know. We can supplement our recipes with them, by introducing dishes that macrobiotics has always used, to balance yin and yang, the cosmic forces man appears to be subject to. Superfoods are also able to bring the world together around the table, even if cooking with common sense would suggest not using too many products brought in from far way, but preferring those obtainable from as near as possible and giving limited room to foods of exotic origin. Above all, it suggests choosing them when they are most ripe: eggplants, peppers, basil in summer, pomegranates, grapes and spinach in the fall, cabbage in winter, broad beans, arugula, apricots in spring. And seeds? The drying process means that cereals and legumes become a vitally important resource at any moment of the year: in winter, especially in soups, broths and hot creamy soups, in salads for cold dishes in the warm months. Here are some periods we should get to know: wheat is at its peak in June; rice between September and October; peas and broad beans in May and June; oats from June to July; mixed berries and wild strawberries in May; black/redcurrants in June; blackberries, blueberries and raspberries in August; figs in August and September. And extra virgin olive oil? Olive picking varies from November to February.

What about seasonings, spices, aromatic herbs? Certainly if they are fresh they can provide generous flavoring, but often, precisely because of the drying process, they concentrate essential oils, minerals and rounded, mature aromas, just those elements which make the difference between a pleasant dish and an unforgettable one.

An important area of superfoods is dedicated to beverages: how can we not mention coffee? Green, not toasted, the distant cousin of the brown, shiny and scented bean, which is part of the everyday rituals for most of us. Well, this beverage, apart from stimulating the nervous system and the metabolism, seems to help in slimming diets. What shall we say about green tea? Certainly an antioxidant. And wine? Anti-aging par excellence, but not only this – it is rich in energy and elements useful for fighting cellular oxidation. Talking about sweets, a teaspoon of malt, rich in the nutritional principles of cereals, is the most recommended resource for vegans, but it is suggested in general for the preparation of cookies and light, healthy cakes, and also for making doughs for bread and savory focaccias rise faster. Finally, the inevitable question: how can we prepare superfoods? In this book we suggest simple recipes, undemanding, fast cooking, consistent with our times and our needs, suspended between work, commitments and our little free time. Appetizing dishes, which can be prepared in advance and consumed at work without losing their freshness and flavor. In the four sections – starters and aperitifs, first courses and single dishes, main courses and side dishes, and desserts, you will be able to find inspiration for super dishes in every sense!

Superfoods
in a nutshell

We should integrate our new foods gradually, watch how our body reacts and see whether we feel tired after eating, then leave the new foods for a few days and introduce the ingredients in minimal doses.

We should vary the dishes every day, trying to have many kinds of food available for our dishes. If we have fresh food resources at hand (for example, from a vegetable garden or an orchard) in the ripening period and not from a greenhouse, let's favor them: this will supply energy and nourishment balanced with the progression of the seasons. Let's try to prepare three large meals and two snacks by distributing fruit, vegetables, carbohydrates, proteins and fats in such a way that the digestive system is spared the stress of being swamped.

We must consider superfoods, especially those that belong to different dietary cultures, a supplement and not the basis of our diet. Let's remember that a balanced diet is varied, colorful, fresh, rich in fragrance. Let's use frozen and preserved foods as little as possible, because the intrinsic properties of foods are reduced by the process of preservation, if not destroyed by long periods of refrigeration.

Let's cut down the consumption of out-of-season foods, let's avoid early produce unless for particular events and let's allow ourselves to be attracted by seasonal products, by their fragrance and their intense colors. Let's try to replace the usual beverages with green tea, non-roasted coffee, organic wine besides being important antioxidants, they do not overload the organism but rather assist it.

Let's try to buy products of declared origin which, even if not exactly organic, come from businesses that pay attention to producing in harmony with the environment, so that they are superfoods both in name and in fact.

Let's favor products that are alive and vital: beans, grains, whole legumes, etc. Let's reduce preparations based on flours unless just ground. Let's try to replace the usual sugar with malt and honey, which have a high sweetening power and a delicious taste and are rich in nutritional substances that are useful for well-being.

GARLIC

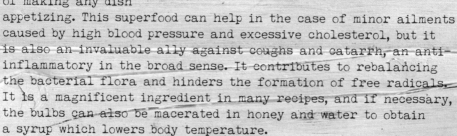

An annual herbaceous plant, rich in properties useful for our well-being, it is a bulb whose presence in the kitchen is capable of making any dish appetizing. This superfood can help in the case of minor ailments caused by high blood pressure and excessive cholesterol, but it is also an invaluable ally against coughs and catarrh, an anti-inflammatory in the broad sense. It contributes to rebalancing the bacterial flora and hinders the formation of free radicals. It is a magnificent ingredient in many recipes, and if necessary, the bulbs can also be macerated in honey and water to obtain a syrup which lowers body temperature.

OATS

These belong to the Gramineae (grass) family. They are refreshing and diuretic, and contain many more proteins than other cereals: oats are therefore indicated for vegetarians and vegans. It is preferable to eat them in winter, owing to their energizing properties. Oats contain minerals such as potassium, calcium, magnesium, phosphorus, zinc, iron, vitamins B1 and B2, PP, D and carotene. You can buy oats in the form of flour and rolled into flakes, both of which are perfect for preparing cookies, cakes, bread, soups, and broths. With a pleasant, sweet flavor, this is the perfect food to fuel children's efforts at school and intellectual work in general.

BULGUR

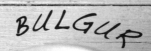

Cracked whole wheat,
you can find it sold
both steamed and
raw; it has the same
characteristics as
wheat grains and can
easily be prepared at
home. It is energizing
and more nourishing
than products based on
refined grains like flour,
pasta, etc. It is the perfect
ingredient for flans, croquettes, soups and salads.
The grain contains calcium, magnesium, potassium,
phosphorus, zinc, vitamins of the B, A, E, K, D, PP
group. It supplies about 319 calories for every 100
grams; it must be avoided by those suffering from
celiac disease because of the presence of gluten.

SWISS CHARDS

This herbaceous plant,
which belongs to the beetroot
family, is extremely rich in water and low in
calories (only 17 calories every 100 grams!).
It is highly digestible, it helps to regulate intestinal
activity, and thanks to the chlorophyll, it contributes
to protecting the organism against tumors and is also
diuretic. Swiss chards contain large quantities of
niacin, folic acid and retinol, vitamin C, vitamin E
and minerals like iron, calcium, sodium, potassium and
phosphorus. Its small leaves are excellent in a salad;
it is ideal lightly cooked for a moment and flavored
with garlic and chili or as an ingredient for savory
pies and flans.

CAULIFLOWER

It belongs to the healthy cabbage group, and is an annual winter plant of which only the central part is eaten. It has low caloric content, but is rich in potassium, phosphorus, calcium and vitamins like vitamin C and folic acid. Thanks to its organic compounds, it performs an action of detoxifying and prevention of tumors. It is excellent if eaten raw in oil dip, and in this way also seems to have an anti-aging function! When you buy it, it must be compact, with no dark patches on the flowers, and it must not smell. Apart from being an ingredient for delicious, tasty recipes, its juice is a great help for fighting illnesses and colds.

KALE

Of all the different types of cabbages, this is the one with the highest percentage of proteins, and it is very nourishing, rich in antioxidants, mineral salts and vitamins (especially C); it is thought to be useful against cancer and to help in detoxifying. Besides being a food with important properties, it is also useful when applied topically to the body for sprains or joint pains. As it has a low caloric content, it is indicated in diets for weight control. It is better eaten cooked, because when eaten raw it can be difficult to digest. Nonetheless, in the United States it is used above all for salads, smoothies and juices.

CABBAGE

There are so many types: the most common are Savoy, white cabbage, red cabbage, Chinese cabbage, etc. Found above all in fall and winter, they are absolutely not to be despised as a food. Recent studies suggest using them because they are anti-cancer. In any case, cabbage seems to be one of the most valuable allies of well-being: it contains vitamin C, folic acid, retinol, phosphorus, potassium, calcium and magnesium. It has a low caloric content (19 calories every 100 grams), and thanks to its organic compounds (like coumarin and phenols) it is an excellent antioxidant and detoxifying agent. It is better to eat it raw or in a salad.

CHICKPEAS

Chickpeas contain good quantities of proteins and sugars and have a high presence of fats. They are magnificent seeds to use when preparing energizing soups, salads and side dishes, but they can be transformed into an excellent flour. They are rich in fiber, help intestinal activity, and contribute to the regulation of cholesterol levels by reducing the "bad" one and increasing the "good" one. They are rich in Omega 3, they contain iron, calcium, potassium, phosphorus, zinc, vitamins C and E, folic acid, and retinol. They are energizing (100 grams supply 334 calories). They are mostly found dried and need to be soaked for at least 8-10 hours before cooking.

BROCCOLI

A low-calorie fall vegetable, it is a real treasure for its antioxidant, cleansing, diuretic, anti-stress properties and is helpful against a sense of fatigue. It seems that it can slow down the process of cellular aging and it is thought that it helps to prevent colonization by helicobacter pylori. It contains 90% water and has a low caloric content (27 calories for every 100 grams); calcium, sodium, potassium, and phosphorus are some of the minerals present. It is rich in vitamin C (100 grams supply half the suggested daily dose). It is excellent eaten raw in oil dip, or steamed or cooked in creams and soups.

POTATOES

Potatoes belong to the Solanaceae family like tomatoes, peppers and eggplants. They can be white and sweet (also called batatas), yellow and sapid, purple, and red. They are still a staple tuber in the diet of many peoples. Digestible, nutritious, rich in starches, they constitute an excellent substitute for cereals since they are, weight for weight, lower in caloric content, stimulate the digestion and regulate intestinal functions. They contain mineral salts - like sodium, calcium, potassium, phosphorus, iron, manganese, copper and sulfur - and vitamins C, K, B group. Potatoes should be stored carefully because the shoots, which grow in case of exposition to light, make them indigestible and slightly toxic.

CARROT

SWEET POTATOES

An edible root whose color ranges from white through yellow, orange, and red, to purple. It is a vegetable containing more than 90% of water, with the substances characterizing it being found in the outer part. The carrot should not be peeled, but washed well and only brushed before use. The root is mineralizing, regulates intestinal function, cleanses the organism, and is anti-anemia, increasing the number of red globules. It is available for most of the year and is the basic vegetable in children's diet. It contains iron, calcium, sodium, potassium, phosphorus and abundant vitamin A.

Solanum lycopersicum, belonging to the solanaceae family, a tomato contains 94% of water. With its 17 calories for every 100 grams, it is a precious vegetable for low-calorie diets, above all in summer! It is rich in lycopene, especially in ripe fruit (very red) and in concentrates, and it helps to reduce the "bad" cholesterol, triglycerides, fights free radicals, and counteracts cellular oxidation. It contains potassium, phosphorus, calcium, sodium, vitamin C, folic acid, and retinol. It is a summer fruit, recommended in that season because it helps us to bear the heat and to lower our body temperature. It must be ripe and firm.

TOMATOES

BELL PEPPERS

With 92% water and only 22 calories every 100 grams, bell peppers are an excellent vegetable to stock up on vitamins without a sense of guilt. They contain a lot of vitamin C, retinol and folic acid and are sold in the shades of green, bright yellow, red and orange. Bell peppers are pleasant to look at as well as good to eat; they are stimulating, digestive, antibacterial, filling, and antioxidant. Because of their relation with chilies, they can sometimes have a hot taste, especially the seeds and the white parts (placenta). They help to fight "bad" cholesterol and protect the cardiovascular system.

QUINOA

Apart from the leaves, which are similar to spinach, the edible part is the seeds, normally used in the form of flour or as grains. It is an energizing, protein-based, and very nourishing food (100 grams produces 368 calories). It is considered as a cereal (because of the high percentage of starch), although it is comparable to spinach and beetroot; it contains all the amino acids essential for our body besides vitamins like B2, C, and E. It does not contain gluten and for this reason it is recommended for those suffering from celiac disease; it is also recommended for vegans and vegetarians for its high protein content. Its flour is excellent for preparing bread, cookies and cakes, while its grains are perfect for flans and patties.

ARUGULA

SPINACH

Autumnal herbaceous plant which contains iron, but above all calcium, sodium, potassium, phosphorus and magnesium and a large quantity of folic acid (vitamin B9), retinol or vitamin A! It is perfect for flavoring tasty salads in the fall, or steamed briefly so as not to lose the precious properties that make it a useful diuretic, mineralizing agent, and antioxidant. It is also indicated as an anti-anemia, the activator of pancreatic secretion and a help for intestinal transit. Spinach is also among the anti-cancer vegetables. It is recommended in children's diets because it stimulates appetite and growth.

JERUSALEM ARTICHOKE

It is an attractive story which characterizes the name of the tuber known as the sweet potato, Canadian potato or topinambur. The Jerusalem artichoke, whose scientific name is *Helianthus tuberosus*, is diuretic, digestive, excellent for cleansing the intestine. In case of obesity, the association with water gives a pleasant sense of fullness, which indicates its use to reduce the quantity of food consumed. It also reduces the absorption of sugars and cholesterol. It is energizing, and recommended for convalescents, old people and children. The Jerusalem artichoke does not contain starch but inulin. It is rich in vitamins A and B and helps in rebalancing intestinal flora.

Arugula, which is both a herb and a salad vegetable, belongs to the *Cruciferae* family; it can be cultivated or wild, and is characterized by a marked spicy flavor and a crisp and tasty consistency. It is perfect for salads or quickly tossed with white meats. An excellent substitute for other salads, or a complement to them, it has digestive and diuretic properties and is recommended for sports people because it helps to lower blood pressure and thus the demand for oxygen. It helps in reinforcing the immune system, has antioxidant properties and also seems to be an ally of the liver.

PUMPKIN

By "pumpkin" we mean fruit with different shapes and colors and very different weights produced by various species of herbaceous plants of the *Cucurbitaceae* family. In general, the pumpkin is rich in water, low in calories (only 18 every 100 grams), a great source of retinol (vitamin A), and of potassium, phosphorus and calcium. Its compact and sugary flesh is refreshing, and has light laxative and diuretic qualities. Its seeds are considered a great help against intestinal parasites. It is a fall and winter vegetable which is perfect in soups and broths, and for the preparation of creams and side dishes.

OREGANO

Full of flavor, appetite-stimulating, digestive: these are only some of the great properties of this herbaceous plant, with a marvelous aroma. It is able to transform a tomato sauce or a pizza into something appetizing and unique. In fact, its fragrance stimulates the secretion of gastric juices and prepares for the digestion. It is a real ally of the digestive process, inhibits possible fermentation in the intestine, and reduces any possible spasms, but it also acts on the respiratory system. Indeed, it can help in the elimination of catarrh. It is the perfect ally for well-being in the kitchen. It can be bought dried or, if you like, it can also be grown in a pot and used fresh.

BASIL

Annual plant with important aromatic characteristics, it can be used in starters, first courses, seasonings and side dishes to make them more appetizing and fragrant. It helps the digestion and also reduces possible stomach or intestine cramps. Basil is an antiseptic, rich in calcium, potassium, phosphorus, retinol, folic acid, and vitamin C. It is a summer plant and in the heat it develops its unmistakable aroma and all the characteristics that make it a precious ally of good cooking for total well-being. In summer, if you rub its leaves delicately on your skin, it also act as a mosquito repellent.

EXTRA VIRGIN OLIVE OIL

It is extremely energizing, with its 900 calories for every 100 grams. It is made up exclusively of fats and elements with considerable anti-oxidizing properties. It seasons, embraces and improves every kind of food and in the Mediterranean cuisine it is the ingredient *par excellence*! It is exquisitely anti-oxidant, it contributes to regulating intestinal transit and to the renewal of cells, it is an excellent anti-inflammatory, it helps to fight free radicals, it improves the appearance of skin, and it reduces the "bad" cholesterol and contributes to the increase of the "good" one. It is better to buy oil from a declared origin, squeezed when cold; it should be kept out of the light, away from heat sources so as not to spoil its balance of nutrients and flavor.

MISO

Miso is a product that can be obtained from soy, barley, rice or wheat; it is obtained by lactic fermentation of seeds in water and salt. It is a compound with great nutritional qualities. It encourages balance in the bacterial flora and is an important remedy in cases of intestinal disorders. It helps in detoxifying, and is useful in cases of excesses of alcohol or food. It contains a large quantity of sodium and therefore should be used with moderation in low-sodium diets. It contains iron, calcium, potassium, phosphorus, zinc, folic acid, and retinol. Miso should not be boiled, but added to broths or soups to season, at no higher than 140 degrees F (60 degrees C) to avoid spoiling its properties.

PINK PEPPER

Despite the name, pink peppercorn has nothing to do with *Piper nigrum* (black pepper): it is a berry, and its size and roundness may remind you vaguely of pepper, but it is decidedly less spicy. The crisp, delicate berries are perfect for gently flavoring the delicate flesh of fish, cream soups, cheese and cereals. It helps the digestion, it is tonic and diuretic, and the berries are also decorative, perfect for making many dishes more appetizing, not covering the flavor but accompanying it. This is a must-have ingredient in new cooking trends, where the colors and beauty of the dish are fundamental.

CHILI

It is unthinkable to not have this magnificent *capsicum* in our diet with its intense, cheerful color and its taste, hot or extra hot according to the type. Apart from its beauty and goodness, it is an ally of well-being, to be used in every season: to help to lower body temperature in summer or to "heat up" dishes in winter! It is antibacterial and anti-inflammatory; it is the fruit with the most vitamin C; it is an excellent source of retinol and folic acid; it helps the digestion; it prevents intestinal fermentation; and in the case of winter illnesses, it acts on nasal congestion, making it less annoying.

BLACK PEPPERCORNS

Pepper seasons, improves and gives its aroma to many dishes: it preserves, brings out appetizing and tasty flavors and is perfect with meat, fish, vegetables and pasta. It is also a friend of well-being that you should not underestimate, as it stimulates the metabolism. It is considered as an antidepressant, since it stimulates the production of endorphins, and encourages the production of heat by the organism. This makes it an invaluable ally for slimming diets, because it helps to burn the calories consumed. Rich in calcium, potassium, phosphorus, vitamin C, folic acid and retinol, its use is not recommended in cases of hypertension and hemorrhoids.

SAFFRON

Rich in lycopene, vitamin A, vitamins B and C, it is a spice derived from *Crocus sativus*, which makes dishes seasoned with its stigmas a magnificent, warm and sunny golden yellow. Just like gold, its price makes it even more precious... also due to what it contains: large amounts of potassium, calcium, iron, sodium, phosphorus, zinc, retinol, B group vitamins, essential oils. It is stimulating, digestive, it improves the mood and stimulates learning and memory. It is a great help for reducing problems connected to the menstrual syndrome.

It is rich in Omega 3 and polyunsaturated fats, and is a great help
in fighting free radicals and slowing down the cellular aging process.
It consists of about 67% water, more than 20% proteins and 11% fats.
It is rich in potassium, phosphorus, sodium, and calcium, and among
its vitamins in particular are folic
acid, retinol, niacin and vitamin
D. It is nourishing and has
a high caloric content:
it contributes 180
calories every
100 grams if
eaten fresh,
and about 140
if smoked, since
it loses part of
the fats in the
process. However, in
the second case, it
is not recommended in
a diet poor in sodium
because it contains a
lot of salt. It is easy to cook and versatile.
It is excellent both raw and cooked.

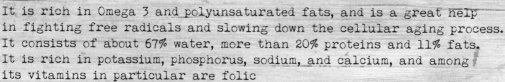

SALMON

Seaweed is an excellent
source of vitamins and there
are many types. Dulse, for
example, is perfect in salads.
Agar-agar, an extract of red
seaweed which is sold in the
form of powder or strands,
is completely natural and
without additives. It is very
useful in diets because it
purifies, is a slight laxative
and it encourages intestinal
regularity. After soaking, the
strands are very pleasant in
a salad, mixed with vegetables
or with other seaweed.

ANCHOVIES

A delicious   small fish which belongs to
the oily fish   category. It is considered to
be one of the   fish which are essential for good
health. In fact,   it is rich in minerals like calcium,
phosphorus,   potassium, sodium, iron, zinc and vitamin
D, retinol, folic acid, and niacin, all useful elements to improve well-being
and good health. The Omega 3s (polyunsaturated fatty acids) present in the
small fish are also useful for reducing the values of "bad" cholesterol and
triglycerides. Anchovies are excellent marinated raw in lemon, fried or stuffed
and salted. The anchovy is an essential ingredient for the "bagna cauda",
an Italian sauce from Piedmont famous all over the world, and particularly
popular in Japan.

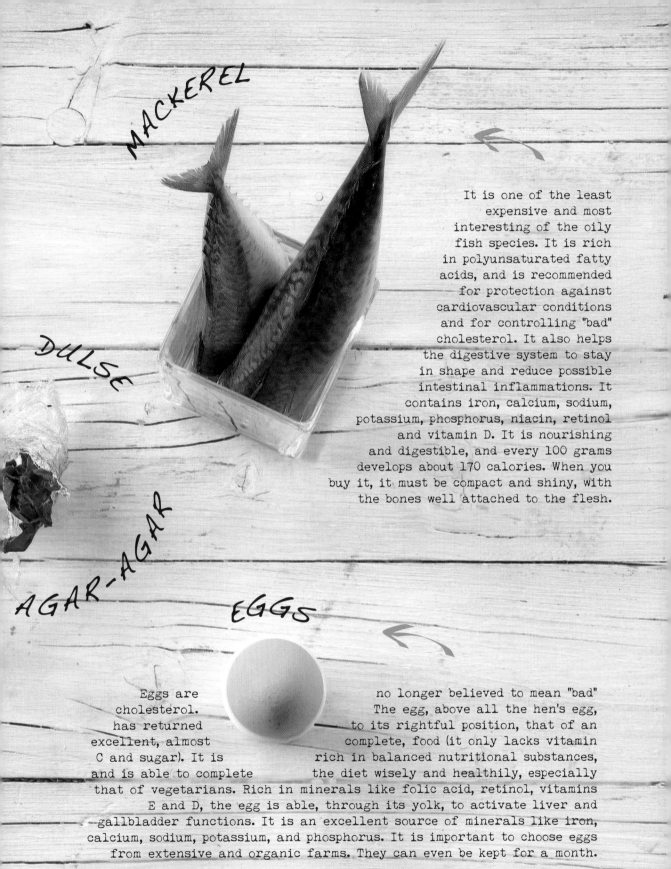

MACKEREL

DULSE

AGAR-AGAR

EGGS

It is one of the least expensive and most interesting of the oily fish species. It is rich in polyunsaturated fatty acids, and is recommended for protection against cardiovascular conditions and for controlling "bad" cholesterol. It also helps the digestive system to stay in shape and reduce possible intestinal inflammations. It contains iron, calcium, sodium, potassium, phosphorus, niacin, retinol and vitamin D. It is nourishing and digestible, and every 100 grams develops about 170 calories. When you buy it, it must be compact and shiny, with the bones well attached to the flesh.

Eggs are cholesterol. no longer believed to mean "bad" has returned The egg, above all the hen's egg, excellent, almost to its rightful position, that of an C and sugar). It is complete, food (it only lacks vitamin and is able to complete rich in balanced nutritional substances, the diet wisely and healthily, especially that of vegetarians. Rich in minerals like folic acid, retinol, vitamins E and D, the egg is able, through its yolk, to activate liver and gallbladder functions. It is an excellent source of minerals like iron, calcium, sodium, potassium, and phosphorus. It is important to choose eggs from extensive and organic farms. They can even be kept for a month.

AZUKI BEANS

The small red beans, which are digestible and purifying, are recommended especially for vegetarians and vegans, but also for people who are simply careful about the food they choose for their diet. They are rich in minerals and micro elements, and have always been part of the Japanese cuisine. Their integration into the cuisines of other nations takes place through the macrobiotic tradition. They are versatile and adaptable, and are perfect for soups, broths, salads and are wonderful in the form of jelly, certainly well known to the admirers of Japanese cooking! They need to be soaked for a night, and to be more digestible, it is advised to add a small piece of kombu seaweed when cooking.

BLACK RICE

BROAD BEANS

This is a herbaceous annual plant of the *Leguminosae*, family. Broad beans can be found fresh in spring and dried throughout the year. Dried broad beans, in particular, are an excellent source of protein and carbohydrates, and rich in potassium, iron, calcium, phosphorus and vitamins like folic acid (vitamin B9) and retinol. They are tonic and energizing due to their fibers, and help intestinal transit. They are an excellent resource in cases of physical and mental fatigue. The fresh legume does not have many calories: about 40, while the dried ones reach 300 calories every 100 grams. They can be harmful for individuals affected by favism.

PUMPKIN SEEDS

These are ideal instead of a snack. They are rich in tryptophan (a precursor of serotonin), which seems able to produce a good mood, and pleasant and restoring slumber, 24 hours powered by natural energy! Pumpkin seeds are also recommended to keep weight under control and they can help in maintaining sugar levels in the blood. They help to reduce "bad" cholesterol, regularize the intestine and supply essential minerals for good health like iron, manganese, phosphorus, zinc, and magnesium, with only 180 calories every 100 grams.

Black rice is naturally fragrant and is particularly appetizing even if simply boiled and served as a substitute for bread. It is also marvelous if oil and salt are added, or it is mixed with the other ingredients to make flans, salads, and omelets. Its anthocyanins are very beneficial in protecting cells against free radicals. It reduces the "bad" cholesterol and increases the "good" one.

CHIA SEEDS

Chia seeds are hispanica, a Lamiaceae family, and Mexico. They a few years due to their for every 100 grams), they improve intestinal transit by gathering toxins like garbage collectors, and they help in cases of irritable colon; they also contain no gluten and are thus recommended for celiacs. They also contribute to maintaining the right blood pressure and are rich in antioxidants. You should not exceed about 25 grams in a day, because Chia seeds could encourage fermentation. In the case of specific pharmacological treatment, it is advisable to contact a doctor before including them in your diet.

small seeds of the Salvia herbaceous plant of the which grows in South America have been in the spotlight for nutritious properties (330 calories

APRICOTS

Soft, velvety, with an enchanting color and melting sweetness, the apricot is an early summer fruit which is perfect for adults and children. It stimulates the defenses of the organism and the appetite in people suffering from loss of appetite; it is a light laxative, and is an important source of vitamins like retinol (vitamin A), folic acid, and vitamin C. Minerals such as potassium, magnesium, calcium, iron, and phosphorus complete this wonderful fruit, which we can also buy dehydrated and in jams. Apricots are perfect if eaten as soon as they are picked (they rot quite easily), cooked in delicious jams or cakes and mixed with other fruit in fruit salads and smoothies. The apricot has a lower caloric content in spite of its sweetness, 28 calories for every 100 grams.

CRANBERRIES

The *Vaccinium macrocarpon* is one of the "essential ingredients" for the preparation of the Thanksgiving turkey. It is a berry which we usually find sold in the form of dried fruit, jam or juice and it is perfect for making smoothies, muffins, cakes and fruit bars. It is rich in calcium, fights osteoporosis, helps with urinary tract infections, can help in cases of degeneration due to arthrosis, and reduces the dangers linked to cholesterol. It has a bittersweet taste and is perfect for making sweets salads, mixed with yogurt or oats and to enrich smoothies and mousses.

FIGS

The fig is a very delicate,
sublimely sweet fruit, which is
rich in digestive enzymes that
help us in the complex work of
assimilating foods; thanks to its
pectin content, it intervenes to lower
the levels of "bad" cholesterol, while
its insoluble fibers contribute to
the regulation of intestinal function.
In spite of this, it is relatively low in
calories (47 calories for every 100 grams).
In addition, calcium, potassium, phosphorus, manganese,
and iron are some of the minerals which, together with vitamins
group A, B and C, make this Mediterranean fruit a superfood
worthy of the name.

MIXED BERRIES

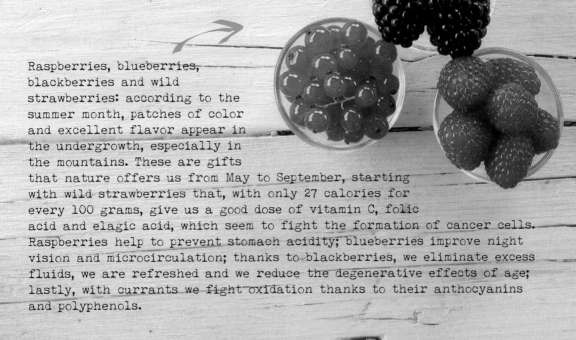

Raspberries, blueberries,
blackberries and wild
strawberries: according to the
summer month, patches of color
and excellent flavor appear in
the undergrowth, especially in
the mountains. These are gifts
that nature offers us from May to September, starting
with wild strawberries that, with only 27 calories for
every 100 grams, give us a good dose of vitamin C, folic
acid and elagic acid, which seem to fight the formation of cancer cells.
Raspberries help to prevent stomach acidity; blueberries improve night
vision and microcirculation; thanks to blackberries, we eliminate excess
fluids, we are refreshed and we reduce the degenerative effects of age;
lastly, with currants we fight oxidation thanks to their anthocyanins
and polyphenols.

GOJI BERRIES

Goji berries, which are antioxidant and anti-fatigue, come from the spontaneous shrub *Lycium barbarum*, present in Mongolia, Tibet, and the Himalayas. They are energizing and nourishing (320 calories for every 100 grams), and so you are advised not to have more than 30 grams a day. In the case of medical conditions and treatment, it is advisable to consult your doctor before including the berries in your diet. They are useful for controlling cholesterol, triglycerides and blood pressure, and they also seem to be a useful food for the prevention of cancer. You can eat them in cakes, cookies, rehydrated and mixed with yogurt, in soups and broths. You can buy the little red berries dried or in juices.

KIWI

An exceptional source of vitamin C, the kiwi is the fruit of the *Actinidia chinensis*, of Chinese origin, which is very successfully grown in many areas of Italy. It is a fruit of the fall, and an extremely useful resource for the winter. Besides vitamin C, it contains folic acid and vitamin E, which contribute to improving your complexion and fighting the action of free radicals. It is extremely helpful in diets because, besides regulating intestinal transit, the kiwi helps to reduce the absorption of fats. Furthermore it contributes to the digestion of proteins. It is excellent raw if eaten alone, and in fruit salads, mousses, and sorbets.

"An apple a day keeps the doctor away," so people say. It is well known that the apple is a fruit of infinite resources, and it regularizes the intestines and the appetite (it supplies 45 calories for every 100 grams). It is a great fresh and juicy snack, particularly perfect in winter when you tend to drink less. It is perfect raw, cooked as a help for intestinal problems, in smoothies, mousses, sorbets and of course as an invaluable ingredient for cakes and sweets. It is better to eat it with the peel, where many of its precious elements are concentrated: calcium, potassium, phosphorus, and good quantities of vitamins C and A.

APPLE

WALNUTS

Five walnuts per day: this is the recipe to help against cholesterol, to reduce the oxidation of cells and to restore a healthy and luminous complexion. Walnuts are an excellent aid for sports people and students. They encourage cerebral activity and are recommended in cases of anemia. Above all, they are made up of lipids and proteins, and are also an excellent source of folic acid, retinol and vitamin E. Among other minerals, the walnut is rich in potassium, phosphorus, magnesium, calcium, zinc, and iron. They are perfect for supplementing the diet of vegans and vegetarians, but they should be eaten in moderation as they have a very high caloric content: 660 calories every 100 grams.

PINE NUTS

Little seeds protected by a shell and a woody pinecone, the fruit of some types of pines, among which also the *Pinus pinea*, pine nuts are above all rich in fats, proteins, carbohydrates and water. They are a great source of potassium, phosphorus, calcium, zinc and folic acid, retinol and vitamin E. They help to fight high cholesterol and maintain blood vessels in good shape. Like all dried fruit, they are extremely high in calories (567 calories for every 100 grams) and they are good for cooking excellent recipes, like, for example, the famous pesto from Liguria. Pine nuts also seem to be able to reduce the sense of hunger, and so are very useful in slimming diets.

PISTACHIO NUTS

Pistachio nuts are seeds which are quite rich in oil and mostly made up of fats, especially unsaturated fatty acids (Omega 3 and Omega 6), proteins and tryptophan, the precursor of serotonin, the good mood enzyme. Recent studies have shown how these seeds help to keep eyes healthy, above all in old people. They reinforce defenses against the attacks of free radicals, fight high cholesterol and are very helpful in improving dry skin and are useful in diets, since their phytic acids reduce the absorption of sugars. Like all dried fruit, they should be eaten in moderation because they are very high in calories (560 calories for every 100 grams).

CURRANTS

A shrub which adorns gardens and vegetable gardens, the *Ribes rubrum* from the *Grossulariaceae* and *Saxifragaceae* families is found wild in mountainous areas. The fruit ripens from June to July, depending on the altitude, and has refreshing, diuretic, slightly laxative and cleansing properties. The main elements of the red clusters are potassium, calcium, phosphorus and a lot of vitamin C. They are perfect for decorating dishes and for making smoothies, desserts, and juices slightly and temptingly sour. These exceptional berries have only 27 calories for every 100 grams: this makes them an extremely interesting addition to a diet.

GRAPES

Good, juicy, sweet, they are the fall fruit *par excellence*. They are nourishing and energizing due to their directly assimilated sugars. They are a great antioxidant and they are considered to be very helpful in the prevention of cancer, thanks to the polyphenols in the skin. Grapes are also able to facilitate intestinal transit, and are diuretic, anti-fatigue, and great for detoxifying in cases of stress. They are marvelous fresh or dried, even if the caloric values for dried grapes are different: fresh grapes supply 60 calories for every 100 grams, while dried grapes supply 283. They contain the minerals calcium, potassium, and phosphorus, and above all vitamins A and C.

For all those who love the food of the Mayas, we should immediately make something clear: its saturated fats do not increase bad cholesterol even minimally, and through the metabolic process it seems that the stearic acid present in chocolate (saturated fat), is transformed into unsaturated fat! The perfect ally with properties which are invigorating, acting against stress, stimulating attention and concentration, it also contributes to skin improvement, making it luminous and soft.
Dark chocolate contains magnesium, which is thought to protect the heart and to be capable of reducing the risks of heart attacks. It also helps to improve the mood in cases of depression.

DARK CHOCOLATE

Beverage, food, medicine, these are a few definitions of this precious liquid with great antioxidants and anti-inflammatory power. One glass of wine per meal, thanks to its polyphenols, helps to fight oxidative stress in cells and seems to reduce cardiovascular risk, the development of tumors and disorders of the automatic nervous system. In addition, of course if it is of good quality and if possible organic, it has benefits for the digestive system, stimulating gastric secretion and the metabolism and helping to counteract the sense of hunger of nervous origin.
A glass of wine (3.4 fl oz/1 dl) develops 90 calories.

RED WINE

MALT

Malt is a sweetener obtained from the germination of cereals like rice, wheat, millet, corn and barley. Those based on rice, millet, and corn are suitable for celiacs. Malt is sold in the form of powder and syrup. It is recommended for vegans, and is an excellent alternative to sugar and honey. It is invigorating and energizing: it is suitable for children's diets, for sports people's diets and for digestive disorders, in that it helps to reduce possible fermentation.
Malt is cleansing and it seems that maltose fights the onset of tumors.
It is the perfect sweetener for preparing cookies and cakes and for improving the rising of all doughs in general, both sweet and savory.

Non-roasted beans have been in the headlines for their slimming properties, true or presumed. Green coffee contains less caffeine, and is less aggressive on gastric mucous membranes; it contributes to controlling cholesterol. It helps to reduce the absorption of fats and also the sense of hunger – this is why it is recommended in diets. As in the case of theine, the caffeine in the bean acts on the central nervous system and favors concentration and good moods, it also stimulates the metabolism. It has an anti-oxidizing action against free radicals and in some cases may alleviate the painful effect of migraine.

GREEN COFFEE

YOGURT

A live food, rich in enzymes useful for our well-being, it is obtained from the fermentation of milk. It is very useful for re-establishing and re-balancing the bacterial flora present in the intestine, it is also easily digested and helps the immune system. It supplies a lot of calcium and has low caloric content (67 calories every 100 grams). Whole natural yogurt can be enriched with fruit, cereals, berries, etc.

GREEN TEA

An evergreen shrub of the *Theaceae* family. Not only are its roasted leaves consumed but in the East it is considered to be not only a beverage, but also a medication because of its important qualities. Tea is a tonic, it is digestive, and it stimulates the nervous system (and is therefore useful for concentration and attention). It is an important antioxidant capable of fighting free radicals. It is extremely rich in potassium, calcium, phosphorus, and zinc, and is very useful for cleansing, drainage and slimming diets, since it helps to reduce the appetite. It is excellent as a hot beverage in winter months or cold, garnished with citrus, other fruit or spices in the summer.

Starters and Aperitifs

At last the aperitif hour, that delightful moment that marks the end of the working day: it is the moment for a drink, to meet with friends before going home or, better yet, to relax over at home with a light meal. Simple dishes, easy to prepare, which also guarantee well-being, rather than leaving a layer of toxins in our organism. How do they do it? With a chickpea purée, we stock up on mineral salts like potassium or phosphorus or vitamins like folic acid, but above all, thanks to the antacid power of the legume, we can digest any reason for stress that has squeezed our stomach. If it is hot, what better than revisiting tomato bruschetta with aromatic coriander? A great idea to fill up with freshness, with 17 calories for every 100 grams, and so much licopene with its antioxidant qualities. Let's not forget to drink a glass of wine, if possible red, to stimulate the metabolism, fight stress, improve the circulation and give so many other benefits. They make the aperitif hour your date with health!

Guacamole

Servings

1 ripe avocado – 1 lime – 1 small onion – 1 ripe tomato – 1 fresh hot chili – 1 tsp of fresh chopped coriander – salt

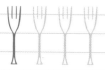

Difficulty

1. Squeeze the lime, peel the avocado and remove the pit, crush it delicately with the prongs of a fork and put the purée in a bowl. Straightaway pour in the lime so that the pulp does not become discolored.

2. Peel the onion, slice it finely and add it to the avocado.

**Prep Time
10 minutes**

3. Wash the tomato, cut it into small pieces, cut off the woody parts near the core and add it to the other ingredients.

4. Season with the salt, chili to taste, the coriander, mix and serve with wafers, small cornmeal mushes or pieces of bread.

**Cooking Time
0 minutes**

Beetroot and spinach with eggs and cheese

Servings

3.5 oz of Swiss chard (100 g) - 3.5 oz of spinach (100 g) - 2 eggs - 1.7 oz of Parmigiano Reggiano (50 g) - 2 tbsp of extra virgin olive oil (about 20 g) - salt and pepper

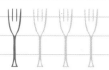

Difficulty

Prep Time
10 minutes

Cooking Time
10 minutes

1. Prepare the vegetables, wash them and soak in cold water for 30 minutes, changing the water several times because spinach often has sand trapped in the leaves.

2. Drain them, dry them, pour the oil into a non-stick frying pan and fry the leaves until they are withered and soft (you need about 5-7 minutes). Drain off any excess liquid.

3. Beat the eggs in a bowl and grate the cheese.

4. Put the frying pan back over medium heat, put in the eggs, add salt and pepper to taste, mix and, when it has thickened (it only takes a couple of minutes), add the cheese, then mix and serve.

Sautéed bulgur with onions, olives and tomatoes

Servings

3.5 oz of bulgur (100 g) – 2 ripe, firm tomatoes – 20 olives – 2 spring onions – 1 lemon – 1 sprig of oregano – 2 sprigs of marjoram – 3-4 tbsp of extra virgin olive oil (about 30-40 g) – salt and pepper

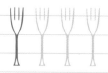

Difficulty

1. Soak the bulgur in cold water for 20 minutes, then wash and boil it in twice its volume of water for 10-15 minutes according to the size of the bulgur. Then drain off any excess water and leave to cool.

2. Wash the tomatoes and spring onions, cut them into small pieces and put them in a bowl; pour in the warm bulgur, add the olives, crumble the oregano, scent with the marjoram, season with the oil, the freshly squeezed lemon, salt and pepper to taste.

**Prep Time
10 minutes**

3. Mix the salad until the ingredients are well blended and serve.

**Cooking Time
10-15 minutes**

Cauliflower and turnip with anchovies and capers

Servings

7 oz of cauliflower (200 g) – 1 turnip – 4 anchovy fillets – 10 capers in oil – rosemary to taste – 1 clove of garlic – 2 tbsp of extra virgin olive oil (about 20 g) – 2 tbsp of vinegar (about 25 ml) – washed cabbage leaves for decoration – salt

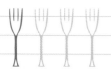

Difficulty

1. Prepare and wash the cauliflower. Wash and peel the turnip, then slice it finely, stew it gently in a non-stick pan with the rosemary and four capers.

2. Add salt immediately so that the turnip releases its juices more easily and cooks better. If necessary, pour in a little water in tablespoons.

Prep Time
10 minutes

3. When the turnip is soft, add the two anchovy fillets, in pieces, and the cauliflower; mix, cook over low heat, with the lid on, for 5 minutes. Take the pan off the heat and plate with cabbage leaves as garnish.

4. Prepare a condiment by chopping the garlic, the six remaining capers, the rest of the anchovies, the oil and the vinegar. Distribute the mixture on the vegetables and serve.

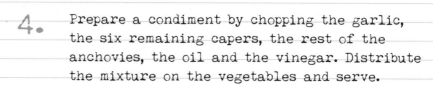

Cooking Time
15 minutes

Millet cream with oat cream, pink and green peppercorns

Servings

3.5 oz of millet (100 g) – 7 oz of oat cream (200 g) – 2 tbsp of linseed oil (about 20 g) – green peppercorn in brine – pink peppercorn – 1 clove of garlic – slices of toast – salt

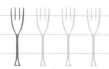

Difficulty

1. Boil the millet in twice its volume of water, with the lid on, for 10 minutes, then take the pan off the heat and leave to cool still covered for an hour.

**Prep Time
10 minutes**

2. In the blender, blend the millet with the oat cream, the oil, and the garlic. Add salt to taste and, when you have a rough but well-blended cream, put it in a bowl and garnish with peppercorns.

3. Serve with toast.

**Cooking Time
10 minutes**

Root vegetables salad with beetroot leaves and broccoli

Servings

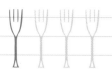

Difficulty

Prep Time
10 minutes

Cooking Time
0 minutes

3.5 oz of very fresh broccoli (100 g) – 10 baby red Swiss chard – 1.7 oz of young chicory (50 g) – 1.7 oz of beetroot leaves (50 g) – 10 radishes – 2 stalks of celery – 2 tbsp of extra virgin olive oil (about 20 g) – 1 tbsp of apple vinegar (12 ml) – salt

1. Prepare all the vegetables. Separately, peel the Swiss chard. If they have good, healthy leaves, add them to the others.

2. Slice the radish, then cut the celery and broccoli into small pieces.

3. Wash and dry the chicory and the Swiss chard leaves, mix and plate them, add all the other vegetables and season with the oil, vinegar and salt to taste.

4. The Swiss chard give a lot of color: cut them and add them to the salad only at the last moment. If you like, you can use them to color the oil for the table, which will turn a magnificent shade of red.

Raw salmon salad with spring onion, lime and coriander

Servings

10.6 oz of salmon fillet (300 g) – 1 spring onion – 1 lime – 6 coriander stalks – 6 salted capers – salt and pepper

Difficulty

Prep Time
10 minutes

Cooking Time
0 minutes

1. Prepare the spring onion and slice it finely. Squeeze the lime juice and sieve it.

2. Prepare the coriander by cutting off the hard parts and chop it. Also chop the capers after desalinating them in cold water.

3. Discard any salmon bones and cut the salmon into small pieces with a sharp knife.

4. Mix it with the spring onion, the lime juice, the capers, and the coriander. Then add salt and pepper to taste (remember that capers maintain a certain taste).

5. Divide the salad into two bowls and serve.

Treat "peperonata"

Servings

2 bell peppers: 1 yellow and 1 red – 1 heaped tbsp of tomato paste (20 g) – 1 onion – 2 tbsp of extra virgin olive oil (about 20 g) – salt

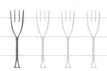

Difficulty

Prep Time
10 minutes

Cooking Time
20-25 minutes

1. Peel the onion and slice it finely. Wash the bell peppers, discard the cores, the white parts and the seeds. Break them up or cut them into little pieces.

2. Pour a thin layer of oil into a frying pan, brown the onion gently and when it is soft add the pieces of bell pepper. Mix and stew, with a lid on, for 5 minutes, then add the paste diluted in half a glass of warm water.

3. Cook with the lid off (about 15-20 minutes), mixing regularly and lowering the heat so that the bell peppers do not burn; add salt to taste and, if necessary, a little water in tablespoons. You can add salt to taste when cooking is finished.

Raw tomato with coriander and spring onion

Servings

14 oz of ripe tomatoes (400 g) – 1 spring onion – 5 stalks of coriander – 1 fresh chili – 1 lime – salt – 6 slices of toast

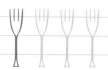

Difficulty

1. Prepare the spring onion, wash and cut it into rounds. Wash the coriander, cut off the hard parts and chop it.

2. Squeeze the lime; cut the chili into small pieces. If they are not irritating, don't discard the seeds, because they make the dish hotter.

3. Wash the tomatoes, cut them into small pieces and cut off any hard part near the cores.

4. Put the pieces into a bowl, garnish with the lime, the spring onion, the chili and the coriander. Add salt to taste, mix and serve with toast.

**Prep Time
10 minutes**

**Cooking Time
0 minutes**

Chickpea purée with spring onion and sesame

Servings

10.6 oz of boiled chickpeas (300 g) – 2 tbsp of extra virgin olive oil (about 20 g) – 1 tbsp + 1 tsp of silken tofu (20 g) – 1 oz of sesame seeds (30 g) – 1 tbsp of lemon juice (15 ml) – 1 fresh spring onion – salt – pieces of toast – black peppercorn (at will)

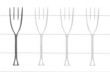

Difficulty

1. Prepare the spring onion by discarding the first outer leaves and cut it into rounds.

2. In the blender, blend the chickpeas with the spring onion, the sesame seeds (set a teaspoon of them aside for decoration), the oil, the lemon, the silken tofu, salt and pepper to taste.

**Prep Time
10 minutes**

3. When you have a thick, smooth and soft cream, pour it into a container of your choice and sprinkle onto it the sesame seeds that you have set aside.

4. Serve the cream with small pieces of hot toast. If you like, make the croutons more fragrant by grinding pepper onto them.

**Cooking Time
0 minutes**

Quinoa flan with bell peppers

Servings

1.7 oz of quinoa (50 g) – 2 tbsp of cornstarch (20 g) – 2 eggs – half a green bell pepper – 1 chili – 0.7 oz of grated Parmigiano Reggiano (20 g) – salt – oil to grease the containers

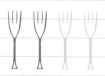

Difficulty

1. Boil the quinoa in salted water and, after about 15 minutes, take the pan off the heat and drain. Leave to cool. Cut the bell pepper into small pieces. Wash and slice the chili.

2. Preheat the oven to 320 degrees F (160 degrees C) and grease two containers.

3. Put the quinoa into a bowl, add all the other ingredients and mix.

4. Transfer into the containers and cook in the oven for about 30 minutes, then take out and serve.

Prep Time
10 minutes

Cooking Time
45-50 minutes

Seasoned yogurt

Servings

13.5 fl oz of whole milk yogurt (400 g) – 2 medium-small cucumbers – salt and black pepper – 1 clove of garlic – 1 lemon

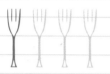

Difficulty

1. Wash the cucumbers, peel them and cut them into small pieces.

2. Peel the garlic and chop it finely. Squeeze the lemon and sieve the juice.

3. Mix the yogurt with the garlic, the cucumber, salt and pepper to taste and add the lemon according to personal taste.

4. Serve with croutons and small pieces of vegetable. It is also excellent as a dressing for salads and a garnish for vegetables in general.

Prep Time
5 minutes

Cooking Time
0 minutes

First Courses
and Single Dishes

For people who want a healthy diet, out-of-home meals are a big challenge. Are superfoods easy to prepare? How can we take a light, healthy dish to work for when we are hungry? There are many dishes that we can cook the evening before, and then transfer into a sealable glass container and heat up for lunch: the cream of broccoli soup, for example, or the fusilli undercooked by 2 minutes, which become perfect the next day, both tossed in a frying pan or heated up in the microwave. Also chicken nuggets can stand the break between cooking and eating. Then there are dishes, like miso soup, which are a perfect symbol of our times: you only need a mug of hot water and a tablespoon of miso, and there you are! A hot and reassuring beverage. You can only keep off your hunger for a time, not for ever, but it is a great help. It detoxifies, balances the intestinal flora and is extremely tasty, besides helping the digestion. Rather than a gobbled panino which you cannot digest, let's not forget that a mug of miso consumed slowly is the best solution and the stomach will feel the benefit!

"Bagna Cauda" with Jerusalem artichoke in oil dip

Servings

5 anchovies - 3.3 fl oz of extra virgin olive oil (1 dl) - 5 cloves of garlic - 1 Jerusalem artichoke - vegetables of your choice like: radishes, spring onions, bell peppers, celery, cabbage, salad etc.

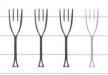

Difficulty

1. Desalt the anchovies, gut them and put them in pieces in a small frying pan with a thick bottom. Peel the Jerusalem artichoke, cut it into small pieces and add them to the anchovies.

2. Peel the garlic and chop it finely, add it to the other ingredients with the oil.

Prep Time
30 minutes

3. Cook until the ingredients become mushy, but without ever boiling the oil (the temperature should never exceed 140-160 degrees F (60-70 degrees C), as burned garlic becomes bitter. You can also cook the "bagna" in a double boiler.

4. After about 40 minutes' cooking over a very low heat, the "bagna cauda" is ready: you can serve it with the vegetables chosen.

Cooking Time
40 minutes

5. The ideal way to enjoy it is to put it in a special earthenware pot (the "fojòt") where you can place a candle in order to keep the food hot.

Cream of broccoli soup

Servings

10.6 oz of broccoli florets (300 g) – 6.7 fl oz of oat cream (200 g) – 2 tbsp of extra virgin olive oil (about 20 g) – 1 tsp of pink peppercorn – salt

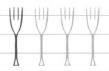

Difficulty

1. Prepare the broccoli, wash it and steam it for about 5 minutes or even more, according to your taste.

2. In a blender, blend it together with the oat cream, season with salt, pink peppercorn, and oil.

3. Heat the cream, if you like it boiling, or serve it at medium temperature. This cream can be eaten with a spoon or on salted wafers, toast or corn flatbreads.

Prep Time
10 minutes

Cooking Time
5-10 minutes

Buckwheat fusilli with chili cream

Servings

5.3 oz of buckwheat fusilli (150 g) – 4 fresh chilies –
1 heaped tbsp of tomato paste (20 g) – 2 cloves of garlic –
4 tbsp of extra virgin olive oil (about 40 g) – salt

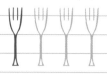

Difficulty

1. Discard the stem of the chilies and, if you want a less strong cream, the seeds (together with the placenta, they are the hottest part). Peel the garlic and blend everything in a blender together with the oil, salt to taste and the tomato paste.

2. Transfer the cream obtained to a tureen and keep it warm.

3. Boil the fusilli in plenty of salted water, following the instruction on the pack. Drain them and put them into the warm tureen, mix with the cream and serve immediately.

Prep Time
10 minutes

4. You can prepare the cream for more than one time. Keep it in the fridge in a container, remembering to cover it with oil.

Cooking Time
15 minutes

Egg and turmeric fusilli with cheese and pepper

7 oz of fresh egg and turmeric fusilli (200 g) – 1 tbsp of powdered turmeric (about 9 g) – 1 tbsp + 1 tsp of butter (20 g) – 1.7 oz of grated Pecorino cheese (50 g) – peppercorn – salt

Difficulty

1. Melt the butter in a frying pan with the cheese. In the meantime, boil the pasta in salted water (if you want to enhance the flavor of the yellow spice, add the powdered turmeric to the water).

Prep Time
2 minutes

2. Fresh pasta cooks very quickly: be ready to drain in 3-4 minutes; move the fusilli with the cheese to the frying pan, mix, make fragrant with plenty of pepper, and serve immediately.

3. Despite the easiness and quickness of its preparation, this first course represents a triumph of fragrances and taste!

Cooking Time
5 minutes

Egg pasta with clams

Servings

7 oz of egg tagliatelle (200 g) – 17.6 oz of clams (500 g) – 0.3 oz of chopped parsley (10 g) – 2 cloves of garlic – 2 chilies – 4 tbsp of extra virgin olive oil (about 40 g) – salt

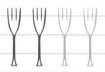

Difficulty

1. Soak the clams into cold water with a tablespoon of salt, let them clean out for a few hours and then ensure that they are all closed with the shell intact. Next, drain them and have them open in a frying pan without seasoning. As soon as they open, take the pan off the heat and sieve the liquid obtained.

**Prep Time
15 minutes**

2. Pour four tablespoons of oil into a suitable frying pan (also to toss the pasta), brown the whole garlic and the chili over high heat, add the parsley and the open clams, mix and take off.

3. Boil the tagliatelle for only a few minutes, drain, and transfer it to the seasoning. Mix and, if you like, heat briefly, pouring in the clams water. Before serving, remove the garlic and the chili.

**Cooking Time
10 minutes**

Garlic and chili chicken

Servings

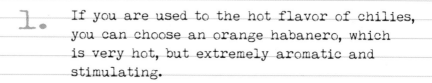

10.6 oz of chicken breast (300 g) - 2 fresh chilies: 1 habanero and 1 tabasco - 10 cloves of garlic - 2 tbsp of extra virgin olive oil (about 20 g) - salt and pepper

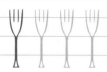

Difficulty

1. If you are used to the hot flavor of chilies, you can choose an orange habanero, which is very hot, but extremely aromatic and stimulating.

2. Cut the chicken breast into pieces. Peel five garlic cloves and slice them, leaving the others whole and unpeeled.

3. Pour into a frying pan the oil, the red sliced chili and all the garlic. Mix and cook for one minute over high heat, then add the chicken.

Prep Time
10 minutes

4. Season with salt and pepper to taste, mix and leave over the heat, adjusting it so that the cooking is lively but not burnt! After about 5-7 minutes, the chicken will be cooked, and you can add the habanero to taste and serve.

Cooking Time
10 minutes

Tomato with peas and tofu

Servings

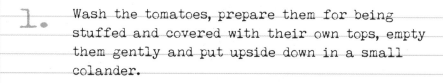

2 large, ripe but firm tomatoes - 3.5 oz of tofu (100 g) -
1.7 oz of peas (50 g) - 1.7 oz of soy (50 g) - 2 tbsp
of extra virgin olive oil (about 20 g) - salt and pepper

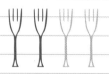

Difficulty

Prep Time
8 minutes

Cooking Time
10 minutes

1. Wash the tomatoes, prepare them for being stuffed and covered with their own tops, empty them gently and put upside down in a small colander.

2. Cut the tofu into small cubes. Put the oil and the peas in a frying pan.

3. Sear over medium-high heat for 5 minutes, then add the soy, salt, and pepper to taste. When the vegetables achieve the desired consistency (10 minutes could be enough), take the pan off the heat and fill the tomatoes.

4. Serve immediately or at room temperature.

Black rice, thyme and cheese

Servings

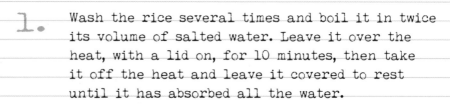

3.5 oz of black rice (100 g) – 1.7 oz of seasoned Toma cheese (50 g) – 4 sprigs of fresh thyme – 2 tbsp of extra virgin olive oil (about 20 g) – salt and pepper

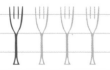

Difficulty

1. Wash the rice several times and boil it in twice its volume of salted water. Leave it over the heat, with a lid on, for 10 minutes, then take it off the heat and leave it covered to rest until it has absorbed all the water.

2. Cut the cheese into two parts: cut one part into small pieces and the other into shavings. Prepare the thyme and remove the leaves off two sprigs.

Prep Time
10 minutes

3. When the rice is ready, season it with the cheese pieces, the thyme leaves, the oil, salt and pepper to taste, mix and serve. Sprinkle the cheese shavings onto the top and decorate with the remaining thyme.

Cooking Time
10 minutes

Filled puff pastries

Servings

2 rice sheets - 3.5 oz of already cooked black rice (50 g) - 3.5 oz of hake fillet (100 g) - 1 egg - 1 tbsp of turmeric (about 9 g) - oil to grease the molds - salt

Difficulty

1. Break up the hake, discard any bones and put it in a bowl with the turmeric, the rice, salt to taste and the egg. Mix and set aside.

2. Soak the rice sheets in warm water till they soften.

3. Preheat the oven to 360 degrees F (180 degrees C). Grease the containers so that after cooking the sheets can be removed without breaking.

Prep Time
10 minutes

4. Remove the sheets from the water, dry them by dabbing gently with a dishcloth and fit them to the container. Then fill them with the hake and cook in the oven for about 10 minutes. Take them out, leave to cool for one minute, turn out and serve.

Cooking Time
10 minutes

Pumpkin flan with pumpkin seeds and tomato

Servings

7 oz of pumpkin already prepared (200 g) – 1 tomato – 3.5 oz of millet (100 g) – 2 tbsp of extra virgin olive oil (about 20 g) – 1.7 oz of soy cream (50 g) – 0.3 oz of pumpkin seeds (10 g) – salt and pepper – oil to grease the molds

Difficulty

1. Preheat the oven to 320 degrees F (160 degrees C).

2. Boil the millet, with a lid on, in twice its volume of water for 10 minutes, then take it off the heat and leave to rest until use.

3. Wash the tomato and slice it. Cut the pumpkin into pieces and steam it until it is mushy, then mash it and put it in a bowl; add the millet, garnish with the oil and the soy cream, add salt and pepper to taste, then the tomato.

Prep Time
10 minutes

4. Grease two serving molds, pour in the mixture, sprinkle the pumpkin seeds onto the top and cook in the oven for 25–30 minutes. Take out, turn out, and serve.

Cooking Time
35-40 minutes

Soy spaghettini with hazelnuts

Servings

2 nest of soy spaghettini (about 5.2 oz/150 g) – 4 tbsp of extra virgin olive oil (about 40 g) – 1 oz of ground hazelnuts (30 g) – 10 fresh basil tips – salt and pepper

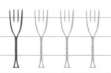

Difficulty

**Prep Time
5 minutes**

**Cooking Time
2 minutes**

1. Wash the basil and dry it by dabbing with a paper towel. Put eight chopped sprigs in the oil and let it absorb flavor for an hour.

2. Sieve the oil and put it in a warm tureen. Add half the ground hazelnuts.

3. Boil plenty of salted water and cook the spaghettini for about 2 minutes. Drain them and transfer to the tureen, mix and flavor with the just-ground pepper and the remaining ground hazelnuts.

4. Serve immediately and decorate the plates with the remaining basil.

Soy, chickpeas and mini shrimps

Servings

7 oz of fresh or frozen soy beans (200 g) – 1.7 oz of boiled chickpeas (50 g) – 3.5 oz of mini shrimps (100 g) – 2 tbsp of extra virgin olive oil (about 20 g) – salt and pepper

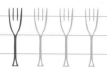

Difficulty

1. Parboil the soy in salted water until you achieve the desired consistency (usually 5 minutes is enough), then drain, pour into a bowl, and add the chickpeas.

2. Pour the oil into a non-stick frying pan, heat it, and pour in the seeds. Mix, add the shrimps, salt and pepper to taste, and mix again. Leave over the heat long enough for the shrimps to go orange, then take them off the heat and serve.

Prep Time
5-10 minutes

3. An excellent dish, perfect when eaten both hot and at room temperature.

Cooking Time
5-7 minutes

Tagliatelle with saffron

Servings

7 oz of egg tagliatelle with saffron (200 g) – 1 spring onion – 1 oz of bacon cut into pieces (30 g) – 6 walnut kernels – 1 pinch of saffron stamens – 2 tbsp of extra virgin olive oil (about 20 g)

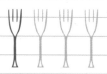
Difficulty

1. Prepare the spring onion, wash it, dry it and slice it finely. Dissolve the saffron in two tablespoons of boiling water. When this is well colored, sieve it and keep the water.

2. Pour the oil into a non-stick frying pan and brown the spring onion; when it is golden, add the bacon, the walnut kernels and the saffron water, raise the heat to the maximum and, when it is half thickened, take the pan off the heat.

Prep Time
10 minutes

3. Boil the tagliatelle in salted water, drain when they are cooked to your liking, garnish with the sauce, mix and serve immediately.

Cooking Time
10 minutes

Miso soup with potatoes, seaweed and tofu

2 tbsp of soy miso (about 20 g) – 1 tbsp of wakame seaweed (about 12 g) – 3.5 oz of solid tofu (100 g) – 1 potato – 1 onion

Difficulty

Prep Time
10 minutes

Cooking Time
10 minutes

1. Peel the potato, wash it and cut it into small cubes. Peel the onion and slice it finely. Put the vegetables together and boil them in a pot with 2 cups of water (about 4 dl) for 10 minutes. Then check to see if they are well cooked. If so, take them off the heat, add the seaweed and leave to cool for 5 minutes.

2. Cut the tofu into small cubes and, when the broth is at about 140 degrees F (60 degrees C) – obtain a kitchen thermometer, which is very useful for so many recipes! – , pour it into the bowls, dilute the miso and add the tofu.

3. It is a very light soup, very useful for the intestinal flora. Miso must never be cooked, boiled or dissolved in a broth which is too hot – or its precious probiotic content will be destroyed.

Main Courses and Side Dishes

Among the superfoods, we must include eggs, extra virgin olive oil, anchovies, salmon and a little red bean: the azuki, the king of beans! Perfect for salads, soups, broths, and also for jellies ... it is a generous, versatile food, which is significant in Japanese and macrobiotic cuisine. Like all dried legumes, it needs soaking before cooking, but that is all you have to remember! Thanks to the richness of flavor of potatoes we can realize healthy and tasty dishes. Whether they are sweet, yellow, purple, it matters little - in fact, let's mix them together for colorful and amusing dishes. Let's go wild with seeds: sesame, Chia, pumpkin, not to mention dried fruits like walnuts, pine nuts and a dusting of spices. Let's use chili both in summer and in winter, for its anti-inflammatory and antibacterial capacity and its energizing qualities. Apart from stimulating the taste buds, it helps us to digest and prevents intestinal fermentation. Let's sometimes add a seaweed salad, one we like: besides being very filling, they are cleansing, detoxifying and mineralizing.

Anchovies with green sauce

Servings

10 salted anchovies – 1 oz of chopped parsley (30 g) – 2 cloves of garlic – 3.5 tbsp of extra virgin olive oil (about 35 g) – 2 tbsp of vinegar (about 25 ml) – pepper

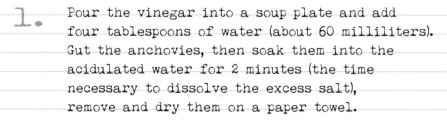

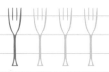

Difficulty

Prep Time
20 minutes

Cooking Time
0 minutes

1. Pour the vinegar into a soup plate and add four tablespoons of water (about 60 milliliters). Gut the anchovies, then soak them into the acidulated water for 2 minutes (the time necessary to dissolve the excess salt), remove and dry them on a paper towel.

2. Peel the garlic and chop it finely, then mix the oil, the garlic and the parsley, add pepper to taste and then add the fillets, mix, and leave to rest for a few hours before serving.

3. Serve the anchovies with toast.

Oat cream with mushrooms and chili

Servings

3.5 oz of seasonal mushrooms (e.g. nail mushrooms) (100 g) – 1 onion – 1.7 oz of millet (50 g) – 7 oz of oat cream (200 g) – 10 cress stems – 2 green chilies – 1 tbsp of grated Parmigiano Reggiano (optional) – salt and black pepper

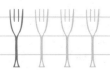

Difficulty

**Prep Time
10 minutes**

**Cooking Time
30 minutes**

1. Wash the mushrooms, cut off the stalks, and cut the heads according to their diameter. Peel the onion and slice it finely.

2. Prepare the chilies and the cress and leave them wrapped in a dishcloth until you use them.

3. Boil the millet and the onion in a pot with 2 cups of salted water (half a liter) over high heat, with the lid off, so that water half-reduces and the seeds and the bulb become completely mushy. Cook for 20 minutes, then add the mushrooms, salt and pepper, and continue to cook over low heat for 10 more minutes, stirring frequently. If necessary and if the soup is too thick, pour in a little hot water (about a small ladleful).

4. Lastly, add the cream, mix and flavor with the peppers (cut into rounds at the last moment) and the cress. Serve hot with some cheese, if you like.

Sesame croquettes

Servings

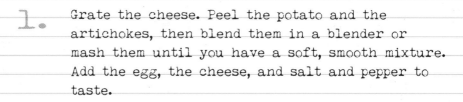

1 boiled sweet potato - 4 boiled Jerusalem artichokes - 1 egg - 1.7 oz of Grana Padano (50 g) - 1.7 oz of sesame (50 g) - 1.7 oz of breadcrumbs (50 g) - 3.3. fl oz of peanut oil (1 dl) - salt and pepper

Difficulty

1. Grate the cheese. Peel the potato and the artichokes, then blend them in a blender or mash them until you have a soft, smooth mixture. Add the egg, the cheese, and salt and pepper to taste.

2. Pour the sesame and the breadcrumbs into a plate, and then mix.

**Prep Time
10 minutes**

3. Make little balls with your hands and coat them in the breadcrumbs. Make them adhere by pressing the croquettes lightly. Heat the oil to 320 degrees F (160 degrees C) and place the croquettes in it. Don't touch them for a couple of minutes, then turn them over. Take them out when they are golden and seem to be solid.

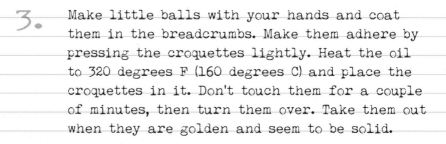

**Cooking Time
6-8 minutes**

4. Put the croquettes on a paper towel to drain off any excess oil. Then place them on a platter and serve.

Azuki bean salad with brown rice

1.7 oz of dried azuki beans (50 g) – 1.7 oz of brown rice (50 g) – 1 carrot – 1 onion – 1 bunch of fresh oregano and basil – 2 tbsp of extra virgin olive oil (about 20 g) – salt and pepper

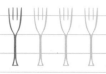

Difficulty

1. Soak the azuki beans for ten hours, then wash them several times and boil them for about 30 minutes. Drain and pour them into a bowl with the oil.

2. At the same time, boil the rice in another pot for 10 minutes in twice its volume of water salted to taste. Then take it off the heat and leave to rest for 30 minutes, with a lid on. If necessary, drain, but normally the rice absorbs all the water.

Prep Time
10 minutes

3. Wash the carrot, if necessary brush it, and cut it into small pieces. Peel the onion and slice it finely.

4. Prepare the herbs, wash them and cut off the hard parts. Mix all the ingredients, season with salt and pepper to taste and serve at room temperature.

Cooking Time
30 minutes

Broad beans and chicory

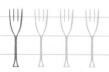

Servings

3.5 oz of dried broad beans (100 g) – 7 oz of chicory (200 g) – 2 chilies – 2 cloves of garlic – 4 tbsp of extra virgin olive oil (about 40 g) – 1 lemon – salt

Difficulty

1. Soak the broad beans for at least 8-10 hours, then wash, drain and boil them in salted water for about an hour, stirring frequently and checking the consistency.

2. Prepare the chicory and sauté it in the frying pan over high heat with the garlic cloves, the chili and half the oil. When it is soft, add salt to taste and take it off the heat.

Prep Time
10 minutes

3. When the broad beans achieve the right consistency (it could take more than 60 minutes), drain them and add them to the chicory, mix and season with salt. If necessary, add more chili and make it taste sour by adding the juice of the freshly squeezed lemon. At last, pour in the remaining oil.

Cooking Time
60-80 minutes

4. It's a perfect dish for versatility: it can be served either hot or cold.

Fantasy omelet with vegetables and black rice

Servings

3 eggs – 4 tbsp of already cooked black rice – 1 section of red bell pepper – 2 fresh chilies – 1 carrot – 2 tbsp of extra virgin olive oil (about 20 g) – salt and pepper – 1 bunch of salad or arugula as side dish

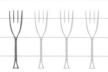

Difficulty

**Prep Time
10 minutes**

**Cooking Time
20 minutes**

1. Prepare the salad, wash it and dry it. Cut the bell pepper into small pieces. Wash, brush and chop the carrot.

2. Pour a tablespoon of oil into a frying pan; gently brown the carrot, the bell pepper, and the pieces of chili. When they are cooked, set them aside and keep covered until use.

3. Beat the eggs in a bowl, add the rice, salt and pepper to taste, the vegetables, and mix.

4. Heat the remaining oil in a custom-made non-stick frying pan, pour in the mixture, turn it several times and cook over low heat for a total of about 4-6 minutes.

5. Place the omelet on a platter and serve it hot with the salad or the arugula dressed at the last moment.

Dulse and agar-agar salad

Servings

1 oz of agar-agar in strips (30 g) – 1 handful of dulse – 1 carrot – 2 tbsp of rice vinegar (about 25 ml) – 1 tbsp of pumpkin seeds (about 10 g) – salt

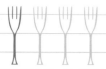

Difficulty

1. Soak the agar-agar into lukewarm water for 5 minutes till it softens.

2. Soak the dulse into cold water for not more than one minute.

3. Wash the carrot and julienne it. Drain the seaweed well, dab it with a dishcloth, add the agar-agar and put everything in a bowl.

4. Add the carrot and the pumpkin seeds, season with vinegar and salt, mix and serve.

Prep Time 10 minutes

Cooking Time 0 minutes

Mackerel, pomegranate and grape salad

Servings

1 mackerel of about 21 oz (600 g) – 2 lemons – 10 grapes –
3 tbsp of pomegranate arils – 2 tbsp of extra virgin
olive oil (about 20 g) – salt and pepper

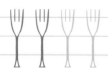

Difficulty

1. Gut the mackerel, discard the head and boil it
for 5 minutes. Then drain it and leave it to
cool. Clean up the fish, removing skin, fishbone
and dark parts.

2. Marinate the fillets obtained for 2 or 3 hours
in the freshly squeezed juice of one lemon.

3. Wash the grapes: just when you prepare the
salad, cut them in two, and break the fillets
into small pieces. Garnish with the pomegranate
and the oil, add salt and pepper to taste. Add
the freshly squeezed lemon juice and mix gently.

4. Divide into portions and serve at room
temperature.

Prep Time
10 minutes

Cooking Time
5 minutes

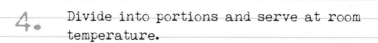

Red and green cabbage and carrot salads

Jars

35 oz of mixed cabbages: red, kale, Savoy, etc. (1 kg) – 2 carrots – 1.7 oz of unrefined sea salt (50 g)

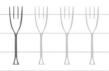

Difficulty

Prep Time
20 minutes

Cooking Time
0 minutes

1. Wash the vegetables well and dry them. Sliced them and, in a container which allows you to mash the vegetables, put a first layer of cabbages, sprinkle in a pinch of salt and continue to make layers and to salt until you have finished the ingredients.

2. Mash the mixture and leave it in a dark place at a temperature of about 68 degrees F (20 degrees C). In two or three days, a liquid forms rich in lactic acid bacteria or milk enzymes.

3. At this point, you can transfer the mixture to sealable jars and keep them in the fridge for one or two weeks.

4. The salads can also be prepared with a suitable press and many vegetables can be used: cucumbers, daikon radishes, turnips etc.

Purple, yellow and sweet potatoes with Castelmagno cheese

Servings

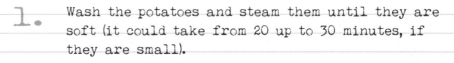

14 oz of potatoes of different colors: purple, white, yellow (400 g) – 1.7 oz of Castelmagno cheese (50 g) – 1 tbsp + 1 tsp of butter (20 g) – salt and pepper

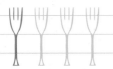

Difficulty

Prep Time
10 minutes

Cooking Time
30 minutes

1. Wash the potatoes and steam them until they are soft (it could take from 20 up to 30 minutes, if they are small).

2. Peel the potatoes, distribute them between two small frying pans and salt to taste. Leave in a warm place until use.

3. Cut the cheese and melt it in the butter over a very low heat: stir frequently so that they blend perfectly. When dissolved, pour the cream onto the potatoes, add the fragrance of pepper, and serve immediately.

Potato patties with Chia seeds

Servings

14 oz of mixed potatoes, both sweet and neutral (400 g) – 1.7 oz of grated Parmigiano Reggiano (50 g) – 1 egg – 1 oz of Chia seeds (30 g) – 1 oz of fine breadcrumbs (30 g) – 3.3 fl oz of frying oil, peanut, for example (1 dl) – salt and pepper

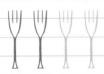

Difficulty

1. Steam the potatoes until they are soft. Try to use potatoes of the same size so that they'll evenly cook. After about 30 minutes, they will be cooked: it is better to peel them when they are hot and mash them straightaway with the prongs of a fork until you obtain a soft, smooth mixture.

2. To the potatoes, add the egg, the cheese, the salt and pepper to taste. Mix until they are well blended.

Prep Time
15 minutes

3. Pour the seeds and the breadcrumbs into a dinner plate, make little balls of your chosen size with the hands, and coat them in the breadcrumbs.

4. Heat the oil in a non-stick frying pan and cook the patties, until well-browned (3-5 minutes is enough). Add salt only when you drain.

Cooking Time
35 minutes

Arugula sautéed with strips of turkey and paprika

7 oz of lean turkey in thin slices (200 g) – 0.7 oz of paprika (20 g) – 3.5 oz of arugula (100 g) – 1 spring onion – 1 tbsp of pumpkin seeds (about 12 g) – 10 cherry tomatoes – 2 tbsp of extra virgin olive oil (about 20 g) – salt

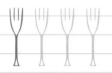

Difficulty

Prep Time
5 minutes

Cooking Time
6-7 minutes

1. Prepare, wash, and dry the arugula.

2. Take 1/3 and put the rest in a tureen, with the sliced spring onion and the pumpkin seeds. Wash the tomatoes.

3. Coat the slices with the paprika, pour the oil into a large non-stick frying pan, and cook them over high heat; after a couple of minutes, add the tomatoes and the arugula, turn down the heat, season with salt to taste and serve with the salad (dressed or not).

Tray of figs with speck and walnuts

Servings

8 ripe but compact figs – 8 slices of speck – 8 walnut kernels – 1 tbsp of honey (about 20 g)

Difficulty

Prep Time
15 minutes

Cooking Time
15 minutes

1. Wash the figs, peel the upper part (the one near the stalk), and cut crosswise. Preheat the oven to 392 degrees F (200 degrees C).

2. Wrap each fig in a slice of speck, place a walnut kernel in the cut, and put them on a round custom-made tray. Distribute the honey over the fruit to flavor it.

3. Cook in the oven for 10-15 minutes, then take out and serve.

Tray of sardines with oregano and pine nuts

Servings

10.5 oz of sardines (300 g) - 1.4 of pine nuts (40 g) - 1 tbsp of dried oregano - 6-8 cherry tomatoes - 2 tbsp of chili oil (about 20 g) - salt and pepper

Difficulty

1. Preheat the oven to 392 degrees F (200 degrees C).

2. Wash the sardines, gut them, discard the heads, and wash them again. Dry them by dabbing them with a paper towel. Distribute a tablespoon of oil into a custom-made tray and put in the sardines.

Prep Time
15 minutes

3. Wash the tomatoes, dry them, cut them into pieces, and distribute them over the sardines. Add the pine nuts, the oregano crumbled, salt and pepper to taste and the rest of the oil.

4. Cook in the oven for about 15-20 minutes, take out, and serve hot.

Cooking Time
15-20 minutes

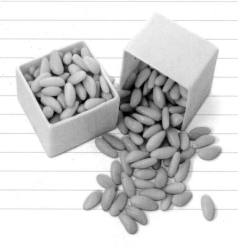

Pickled vegetables with red sauce and green cauliflower

Servings

1 bell pepper – 1 zucchini – 2 sticks of celery – 2 carrots – 7 oz of Romanesco (200 g) – 6 tbsp + 1 tsp of apple vinegar (1 dl) – 10.5 oz of canned tomatoes in pieces (300 g) – salt and pepper

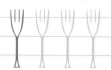

Difficulty

Prep Time
20 minutes

Cooking Time
20 minutes

1. Prepare all the vegetables, wash them, dry them and cut them into pieces (leaving them all separate). Give rein to your imagination.

2. Heat 4 cups of water (one liter) with the vinegar. When it boils, first cook the carrots and the celery for 7 minutes, drain and let evaporate; then cook the zucchini for 5 minutes, the bell pepper for 3-4 minutes, and lastly the cauliflower for 3 minutes.

3. When the vegetables have been drained well, pour the tomato into the frying pan, add all the other vegetables, add salt and pepper to taste, and cook for 2-3 minutes over medium heat.

4. When the vegetables are well browned, you can serve them at room temperature or put them in jars, and after sterilization preserve them in a dark, cool place.

Fruit
Desserts

Fresh fruit and still more fruit, but seasonal, ripe and fragrant, then dried either berries or nuts: these are the superfoods that make a dessert a dish with vitamins, mineral salts, antioxidants ....just think of grapes - they are detoxifying, they help in fatigue, they help to drain. Kiwis can fill you up with vitamin C, while caressing cocoa can help you maintain concentration and immediately replenish the reserve of energy. If you mix millet flakes and oats with a tablespoon of just-melted dark chocolate you immediately have a tasty bar, to take a break or recharge your energy. Let's go back to country ways, enjoying grape and figs bread: it is simple to prepare and an excellent substitute for shop-bought snacks and bars! With Goji berries, from the valleys of the Himalayas, we reduce tiredness by preparing mini muffins to eat when we lack energy. With mixed berries, sautéed for a moment in the frying pan with a tablespoon of malt and one of water, we garnish silken tofu to obtain a delicious and healthy dessert, which is easy to digest, and also perfect for vegans and people intolerant to dairy products.

Apricots in preserve with spices

14-oz jars

35 oz ripe but compact apricots (1 kg) – 1 small cinnamon stick – 10 cardamom pods – 1 tbsp of pink peppercorn – 2 tbsp of brown sugar (about 30 g)

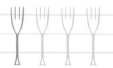

Difficulty

Prep Time
20 minutes

Cooking Time
25 minutes

1. Wash the apricots, divide them into two parts and remove the kernels. Crush the cardamom in a mortar to open the pods, break up the cinnamon.

2. Pour the sugar into a frying pan, melt it over low heat, add the spices and the apricots, then pour in 4 tablespoons of water. Raise the heat and cook for one minute.

3. Put into jars, pressing the fruit gently, pour in the syrup, close and sterilize the jars by boiling them in water for 20 minutes wrapped in dishcloths.

4. Leave to cool and, when the vacuum forms, you can place the jars in a cool, dark place and keep them for months.

Walnut and chocolate cookies

Servings

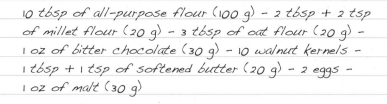

10 tbsp of all-purpose flour (100 g) - 2 tbsp + 2 tsp of millet flour (20 g) - 3 tbsp of oat flour (20 g) - 1 oz of bitter chocolate (30 g) - 10 walnut kernels - 1 tbsp + 1 tsp of softened butter (20 g) - 2 eggs - 1 oz of malt (30 g)

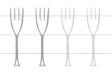

Difficulty

1. Crush the walnuts in a mortar. The more delicate this phase is, the less buttery the result will be. Break up the chocolate and place both the ingredients in a bowl.

2. Mix the flours with the eggs, the butter, the malt and lastly the walnuts and the chocolate, but only when the mixture is smooth and well blended.

Prep Time
20 minutes

3. Preheat the oven to 350 degrees F (180 degrees C) and line a baking tray with parchment paper.

4. Lay out the dough on a floured surface, and with a round cookie cutter, make disks of about 2-3 inches in diameter. Place them on the tray. Cook in the oven for 10-15 minutes and leave to cool before serving.

Cooking Time
10-15 minutes

Chocolate with cereals and pistachios

Servings

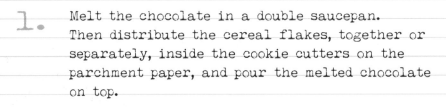

7 oz of bitter chocolate (200 g) – 2 tbsp of puffed millet (about 15 g) – 2 tbsp of rolled oats (about 11 g) – 2 tbsp of crumbled pistachios (about 17 g)

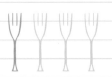

Difficulty

Prep Time
10 minutes

Cooking Time
5 minutes

1. Melt the chocolate in a double saucepan. Then distribute the cereal flakes, together or separately, inside the cookie cutters on the parchment paper, and pour the melted chocolate on top.

2. Proceed in the same way with the pistachios. Before you serve them, leave to set in the fridge for at least 2 hours. Take the chocolates out of the cutters and serve.

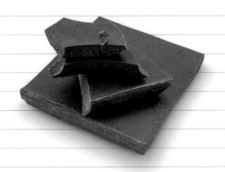

Shot glass cream with raspberries and currants

Servings

10.5 oz of silken tofu (300 g) – 10.5 oz of currants and raspberries (300 g) – 1 tbsp of malt (about 20 g) – 1 lemon

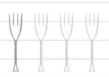

Difficulty

Prep Time
10 minutes

Cooking Time
0 minutes

1. Prepare the fruit, wash it and dry it, by dabbing it gently.

2. Crush half the fruit and collect the juice obtained; add the just-squeezed lemon, and mix with the malt until you obtain a well-blended syrup.

3. Divide the silken tofu between two glasses, pour in the remaining fruit, flavor with the juice, and serve.

4. The dessert can also be served cold after setting in the fridge for a couple of hours.

Kiwi cream with soy whipped cream and pomegranate

Servings

2 kiwis – 1 lemon – 7 oz of soy whipped cream (200 g) – 2 tbsp of Acacia honey (about 30-40 g) – 1/2 small pomegranate

Difficulty

1. Peel the kiwis, cut them into pieces and put them into the blender. Squeeze the lemon and add it to the fruit, together with the honey.

2. Blend the mixture until you obtain a fluid cream, pour it into a bowl, add the soy cream and blend it into the fruit with a whisk.

3. Leave to rest in the fridge for an hour. In the meantime, prepare the pomegranate arils.

4. When you serve, distribute the cream into two glasses and decorate with arils.

Prep Time
20 minutes

Cooking Time
0 minutes

Apple and blueberry crumble

Servings

5 tbsp of all-purpose flour (50 g) – 3 tbsp + 1 tsp of butter (50 g) – 2 red apples – 2 tbsp of cranberries (about 14 gr) – 1.7 oz of fresh blueberries (50 g) – 2 tbsp of brown sugar (about 30 g)

Difficulty

1. Peel the apples and wash the blueberries. Grease a small baking tray with butter and preheat the oven to 390 degrees F (200 degrees C).

2. Cut the apples into small pieces and put a layer of them on the baking tray, dust with part of the flour, distribute some blueberries, some cranberries, some pieces of butter and some sugar, setting aside some of them for the second layer. Repeat with the ingredients that you have set aside until they're finished and then place in the oven.

3. Cook for about 20 minutes, then take out and serve hot or lukewarm.

Prep Time
15 minutes

Cooking Time
20 minutes

Date, dried fig, cranberry and pistachio roll

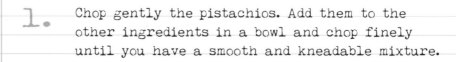
1 small sheet of Carasau flatbread – 6 dried figs – 6 dates – 10 pistachios – 10 cranberries

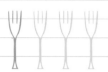

Difficulty

Prep Time
15 minutes

Cooking Time
0 minutes

1. Chop gently the pistachios. Add them to the other ingredients in a bowl and chop finely until you have a smooth and kneadable mixture.

2. Soak the Carasau in cold water for 30 seconds, then take it out, lay out on a dishcloth, and leave it to rest for 5 minutes, turning it once.

3. When the Carasau is dry, but soft, spread on the cream, roll it up, cut into rounds with a very sharp knife, and serve.

Mixed berry lasagne

Servings

3.5 oz of egg lasagna sheets (100 g) – 7 oz of mixed berries, according to the season (200 g) – 7 oz of vegetable cream (200 g) – 1 tbsp of brown sugar (about 15 g)

Difficulty

1. Prepare the fruit, wash it and leave it on a dishcloth to dry.

2. Mel the sugar and half the fruit cooking them gently over low heat in a non-stick frying pan; when they are flaked off, add the cream, take the pan off the heat and mix again.

3. Cut the sheets into small squares and toast them in a hot non-stick frying pan, so as to obtain crisp lasagne.

Prep Time
15 minutes

4. Make up the lasagne by distributing the crisp sheets, the cream, and the fruit. Then serve.

Cooking Time
10 minutes

Muffins with Goji berries

6-8 muffins

8 tbsp of all-purpose flour (80 g) – 7 tbsp of millet flour (50 g) – 3 tbsp + 2 tsp of oat flour (20 g) – 1 oz of Goji berries (30 g) – 2 tbsp of melted butter (30 g) – 1 oz of malt (30 g) – 2 eggs – 1.7 fl oz of apple juice (0.5 dl) – 1 tsp of baking powder for desserts (4 g) – butter or cooking spray for molds

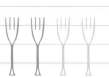

Difficulty

1. Preheat the oven to 320 degrees F (160 degrees C) and grease the muffin molds.

2. Soften the Goji berries in hot apple juice for 5 minutes, then drain, setting the juice aside. Dissolve in it the baking powder and the malt.

Prep Time 20 minutes

3. Mix the flours with the eggs and the butter, and add the apple juice. When you have a soft, smooth mixture with no lumps, add the berries.

4. Divide the mixture into the molds and cook in the oven for about 20-30 minutes. Then take out and leave to cool before serving.

Cooking Time 20-30 minutes

Bread with grapes and figs

Servings

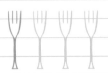

Difficulty

Prep Time
10 minutes

Cooking Time
20-30 minutes

1/2 cup + 3 tbsp of all-purpose flour (150 g) - 2 tbsp of extra virgin olive oil (about 20 g) - 4 ripe figs - 20 black grapes - 1 scant tsp of baking powder for savories (3 g) - salt

1. Wash the fruit, take the grapes off the stalk, discard the stem of the figs and cut them into four parts.

2. Put the flour in a bowl, add the salt, the oil and the baking powder, and little by little pour in about 1/3 cup (0.75 dl) of water. Mix until all is blended and smooth, and leave to rise covered for about 30 minutes, while you preheat the oven to 390 degrees F (200 degrees C).

3. Cover a baking tray with parchment paper. Lay out the risen dough on the baking tray and distribute the fruit according to your personal taste.

4. Cook in the oven for 20-30 minutes. Then take out of the oven, leave to cool, and serve.

Lemon sorbet with white wine

Servings

5 lemons - 0.8 fl oz of white wine (0.25 dl) and a glass to serve - 2 tbsp of caster sugar (about 25 g) - 5 sage leaves

Difficulty

Prep Time 40 minutes

Cooking Time 0 minutes

1. Boil 2 tablespoons of water (about 0.25 dl) with the sugar and the sage, and leave to cool. Squeeze the lemon and sieve the juice. Set some sage and lemon aside for decoration.

2. Mix the lemon juice, the sugar syrup and the wine. Place in the ice-cream freezer for 30 minutes until is frozen.

3. When you come to serve the sorbet, share it among those present, dilute it with the wine that you have set aside, and decorate with sage and lemon.

Pistachio cake

Servings

1.8 oz of chopped Bronte pistachios (50 g) – 4 dried figs – 10 boiled chestnuts – 0.7 oz of toasted sesame seeds (20 g) – 1 oz of bitter chocolate (30 g)

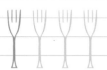

Difficulty

Prep Time
15 minutes

Cooking Time
0 minutes

1. Chop up the chocolate with a sharp knife until you have very small, irregular pieces. Peel the chestnuts.

2. In a blender, blend the figs and the chestnuts until you obtain a mixture that is smooth and kneadable but consistent. Add the toasted sesame and the chocolate, and mix until the ingredients are well blended.

3. Make a tower of the dough using a moistened cylinder (ring, but higher), take it gently from the mold and cover it with the chopped pistachios.

4. Leave the cake to set for an hour in the fridge, then slice and serve.

Malt flan with cranberries and kiwi

Servings

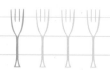

5 tbsp of all-purpose flour (50 g) – 7 tbsp of millet flour (50 g) – 5 tbsp of cornstarch (50 g) – 2 eggs – 1 oz of malt (30 g) – 1.7 fl oz of apple juice (0.5 dl) – 1 kiwi – 0.7 oz of cranberries (20 g) – 3 tbsp of corn oil (about 30 g) – 1 tsp of baking powder for desserts (4 g) – butter spray or oil to grease the containers

Difficulty

1. Preheat the oven to 350 degrees F (180 degrees C). Grease two individual oven containers. Peel the kiwi, and cut it into small pieces or slices.

2. Soak the cranberries in warm apple juice till they soften. Then drain them, and dissolve the malt and the baking powder in the liquid. Mix the flours with the eggs; add the apple juice and the oil.

3. Work the ingredients until you have a smooth mixture, and add the fruit. Divide the mixture in two containers and cook in the oven for 20-25 minutes; then leave to cool and serve.

Prep Time
10 minutes

4. You can serve the cake with green coffee.

Cooking Time
20-25 minutes

Red wine with spices

Servings

6.8 fl oz of full-bodied red wine (2 dl) – 1 small cinnamon stick – 4 cloves – 5 cardamom pods – some pieces of organic lemon zest – optional: 2 tsp of chestnut honey (about 14 g)

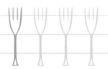

Difficulty

1. Crush the cardamom pods delicately, break up the cinnamon and cut the lemon zest into small pieces.

2. Heat the wine until it boils and take it off the heat. Add all the ingredients (except the honey), leave to infuse for 2 minutes, sieve, sweeten with honey, if you like it.

3. This excellent beverage for the winter warms, stimulates perspiration and is useful for colds.

Prep Time
5 minutes

Cooking Time
5 minutes

The author

CINZIA TRENCHI is a naturopath, journalist, and freelance photographer. She specialized in nutrition and enogastronomic trails, and collaborates on many cookbooks from publishers in Italy and abroad. A passionate cook, she has worked for many years with various Italian magazines, revisiting regional, traditional, macrobiotic and natural cooking specialities, supplying content and photographs and suggesting dishes she has conceived. Her cookbooks propose original and creative diets, associating flavors and trying out unusual combinations that give rise to new dishes inspired by taste. She always remembers the nutritional characteristics of the foods to achieve a greater balance at table and a consequent improvement in well-being. She lives in in Montferrat, in Piedmont, in a house deep in the country. She prepares sauces and original condiments with flowers, herbs, and the produce from her vegetable garden, which she also uses to decorate her dishes. She is guided by the seasons and her knowledge of the fruits of the earth. White Star Publishers has published these books by her in English: "Gluten-Free Gourmet Recipes"; "Fat-Free Gourmet Recipes"; "Chili Pepper: Moments of Spicy Passion"; "My Favorite Recipes", "Smoothies & Juices: Health and Energy in a Glass", "Mug Cakes: Sweet and Savory Recipes" and "Detox, Practical Tips and Recipes for Clean Eating".

Index of Ingredients

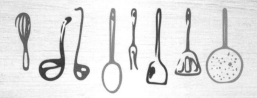

WS White Star Publishers® is a registered trademark
property of De Agostini Libri S.p.A.

© 2016 De Agostini Libri S.p.A.
Via G. da Verrazano, 15
28100 Novara, Italy
www.whitestar.it – www.deagostini.it

Translation: Jonathan West, Kathryn Lake
Editing: Iceigeo, Milano (Margherita Giacosa, Paola Paudice, Giulia Gatti)

ISBN 978-88-544-1021-3
1 2 3 4 5 6   20 19 18 17 16

Printed in China

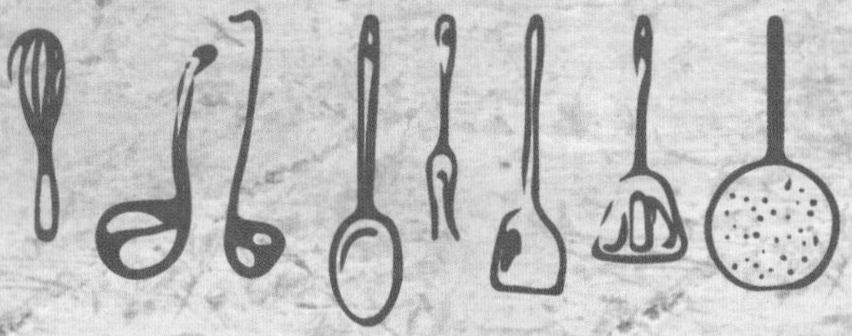